T3-BUX-516

HORS D'OEUVRES

Who knows better than a diplomat's wife how much a tasty and well-prepared hors d'oeuvre can contribute toward the success of a party—or how important it is that parties be successful? And who else but a large group of Foreign Service ladies like the authors of this book, who have traveled and lived and given parties in all parts of the world, could have made such a varied collection of mouth-watering recipes?

The recipes come from many lands and many of them have until now been jealously guarded secrets. Each has been individually tried and tested many times, and only those have been included which passed rigid tests of tastiness and easy preparation. Charmingly illustrated in color, written in a concise, easy-to-follow style, and with a foreword by Mrs. Douglas MacArthur II, wife of the American Ambassador to Japan, the book describes hors d'oeuvres that are sure to please the most fastidious of gourmets, to titillate the most jaded of palates—and to bring thousands of miles of travel and exotic cooking to the hostess's cocktail table.

HORS D'OEUVRES

Favorite Recipes from Embassy Kitchens

by the Women's Club of the U. S. Embassy, Tokyo

Shom Atkin Edmond : Editor
Virginia Jacobs McLaughlin : Illustrator

CHARLES E. TUTTLE COMPANY
RUTLAND, VERMONT & TOKYO, JAPAN

Representatives
Continental Europe: BOXERBOOKS, INC., Zurich
British Isles: PRENTICE-HALL INTERNATIONAL, INC., London
Australasia: PAUL FLESCH & CO., PTY. LTD., Melbourne
Canada: HURTIG PUBLISHERS, Edmonton

Published by the Charles E. Tuttle Company, Inc.
of Rutland, Vermont and Tokyo, Japan
with editorial offices at
Suido 1-chome, 2-6, Bunkyo-ku, Tokyo

Copyright in Japan, 1959
by the Charles E. Tuttle Company, Inc.

Library of Congress Catalog
Card No. 59-8190

International Standard Book No. 0-8048-0254-8

First printing, 1959
Fifteenth printing, 1974

Printed in Japan

Contents

The honor of being chosen to write the foreword for "*Hors D'Oeuvres: Favorite Recipes from Embassy Kitchens*" is not without a certain irony. Life early forced a choice upon me, the choice between food or figure. And, wisely I think, I chose the latter—with its concomitant advantages of husband and clothes.

So, although I have read this book with mouth-watering avidity, I'm sorry to say that its sole personal use will be as a lure to my less-disciplined friends.

And what a lure it is! No more tempting or varied array of canapés could ever be collected in one volume. The American Embassy Women's Club of Tokyo, Japan, has compiled recipes to titillate the appetite of the most demanding gourmet. There are recipes from all over the world, bringing memories of reflections on glistening Paris boulevards, of the approach of fall in New England, of cherry-blossom time in Japan, of the Taj Mahal by moonlight .... It is truly a culinary travelogue.

The motivation behind this volume, compiled with the able and encouraging support of Mr. Meredith Weatherby, Editor-in-Chief of Charles E. Tuttle Company, is one of high purpose and warm fellowship. It is to further international understanding and friendship through closer communion of all peoples of the world. Believing that the appreciation and enjoyment of the delicacies of each other's country will enhance the rapport between nations, the American Embassy Women's Club has compiled this book.

The Club, during its six years of existence has provided three scholarships to Japanese students in the universities of Tokyo and Kyoto, has helped support a nursery school, has made it possible for a Fulbright scholar to go to the United States, has made financial gifts when sudden disasters befell Japan, and has aided the Consulates in their charity work. It is hoped that the publication of this book will enable us to continue and enlarge these and other activities.

My warmest congratulations to all who contributed to this tempting project.   May your friendship increase —but not your figures.

Laura Barkley MacArthur
(Mrs. Douglas MacArthur II)

U. S. Embassy
Tokyo, Japan

ANGELS & ON HORSEBACK

Usually served as a savoury in England as the final course.

2 doz. oysters, raw
1 tbsp. lemon juice
cayenne

8 strips bacon, cut into thirds
minced parsley

Season oysters with lemon juice and dash of cayenne. Wrap in bacon and secure with toothpicks. Sprinkle with minced parsley. Place on shallow dish and bake in hot oven (450°) until bacon is crisp. Serve on buttered toast.

Another version of this often served in Japan: substitute smoked oysters for raw oysters. Omit seasoning. Delicious!

Keep one of these in the refrigerator for unexpected guests.

1 small Gouda cheese
2 tbsps. beer
1 tsp. Worcestershire sauce
dash tabasco

Cut a wide circle in the top of the Gouda. Remove red skin (on top only) and scoop out cheese, leaving a firm shell. Let scooped cheese stand at room temperature. Mash cheese with a fork and add other ingredients. Let mixture stand for another hour. Put back into shell and chill. (Flavor is improved if mixture is allowed to age for a few days.) Surround with black bread or crackers and let guests serve themselves.

SHERRY CHEESE SPREAD

Nice to have on hand.

1/2 lb. cheddar cheese, grated
1 1/2 oz. dry sherry
1 tbsp. brandy
1/8 tsp. Worcestershire sauce

Cream the cheese, sherry, and brandy together. Add Worcestershire sauce. Cream again. Put into crock and chill for at least 1 day to age. Serve with crackers or unsalted biscuits. Mixture will keep for at least a month.

Makes about 1 cup.

DUTCH TRUFFLES

The flavor reminds us of rarebit,
but the texture is quite different.

2 cups grated Gouda or Edam cheese
1 to 2 tbsps. cream or ale
1/4 tsp. dry mustard
1/4 tsp. salt
1/8 tsp. pepper
1/4 cup finely chopped celery
1/4 cup finely chopped parsley

Mix grated cheese and chopped celery together. Add mustard, salt, and pepper. Add enough cream or ale to make mixture firm enough to mold. Mix well. Form this into balls about the size of a marble and roll in chopped parsley. Chill before serving.

Makes approximately 60 balls.

Very cool looking for use
as summer hors d'oeuvres.

1/4 lb. blue cheese
1/4 cup coffee cream
1/2 cup heavy cream

Press cheese through fine sieve. Add coffee cream and mix thoroughly. Place into top of double boiler and stir until smooth. Remove from heat. Chill. Beat in heavy cream. Place inside shallow mold and freeze 4 hours or until mousse is firm. Unmold onto chilled serving dish and surround with rounds of dark bread. The mixture will keep for about 1 week.

Makes about 1 cup.

CHICKEN LIVER MOUSSE

*Make this spread at your
leisure and keep it on hand.*

5 chicken livers
1 tbsp. butter
2 tbsps. tomato catsup

2 tbsps. whipped cream
salt and pepper to taste
rounds of bread

Sauté the livers in butter. Remove from skillet and chop finely. Season with salt, pepper, and tomato catsup. Return mixture to skillet and cook for a few minutes. Allow to cool. Put through a fine sieve and fold into the whipped cream. Cut thin pieces of bread and fry them in salad oil. Remove from skillet and place on absorbent paper. Place spread on the fried bread with decorating tube.

The spread may be made in advance and refrigerated for several days or kept in the freezer.

Makes approximately 25 canapés.

Guaranteed to please
any lover of pâté

1/2 lb. chicken livers	*pinch cayenne*
2 tbsps. onion, grated	*1/4 tsp. nutmeg*
1/2 cup chicken fat (*rendered*)	*1 tsp. dry mustard*
or softened butter	*1/8 tsp. ground cloves*
1/2 tsp. salt	

Drop chicken livers into just enough boiling water to cover and simmer, covered, for 15 minutes. Drain well. Put simmered livers through finest blade of a food chopper or through a food mill 3 times. Add remaining ingredients and blend well. Pack into a crock or small glass jar and store in refrigerator for 12 hours, at least.

The mixture will keep for about 1 week, if you can stay away from it that long.

Makes about 1 cup.

PUFF SHELLS

These are very easy to prepare, quite attractive, and extremely useful. They can be made days ahead of time or months ahead and frozen. When ready to use just fill them with one of your favorite fillings or one of those found within these pages.

1/4 cup shortening	*1/4 tsp. salt*
1/2 cup boiling water	*2 eggs*
1/2 cup sifted enriched flour	

Melt shortening in the boiling water. Sift the flour and salt together and add them to the shortening and water all at once, stirring constantly. Cook until mixture leaves sides of pan in a smooth ball. Remove from heat, cool for about 1 minute. Add the eggs 1 at a time, beating thoroughly after each addition until mixture is smooth again. Drop by 1/2 teaspoonfuls on greased baking sheet. Bake in hot oven (475°) for 7 to 8 minutes (until points begin to brown), then reduce heat to 400° for 10 to 12 minutes. When cold, cut the top off, fill, and replace the top over the filling. We suggest Sardine Cream (page 35) or Crabmeat Delight (page 90) as delicious fillings.

Makes 36 small puffs.

SCALLOPS ON SKEWERS.

An Epicurean delight.

1/2 lb. scallops, washed, drained, quartered
1 cup dry white wine
3 sprigs parsley
1 bay leaf
1/2 tsp. salt
1/8 tsp. pepper
3 strips bacon, partially cooked

Bring to a boil the wine, parsley, bay leaf, salt, and pepper. Add the scallops and simmer for 5 minutes. Drain. Alternate squares of bacon and scallops on skewers. Place skewers on a lightly buttered baking pan and bake slowly until bacon is crisp.

These may be prepared in advance and put in the oven at the last minute.

Makes about 30 hors d'oeuvres.

Stuffed mushrooms

The most discriminating mushroom fancier will take off his hat to you for these.

1 lb. fresh mushrooms
1 tbsp. chopped scallions
1 tbsp. butter
1/2 pint whipping cream
1 tbsp. sherry
1/2 tsp. salt
1/8 tsp. pepper

Wash and dry mushrooms. Remove stems and chop them very finely. Sauté minced mushroom stems and chopped scallions in the butter. Add the cream, sherry, salt, and pepper. Cook until mixture thickens, about 10 minutes. Fill caps of the mushrooms with the filling and broil until brown and bubbling.

These may be prepared in advance and refrigerated or frozen to be popped under the broiler just before serving.

Makes approximately 30 mushrooms.

These are not only delicious, but are among the
loveliest looking hors d'oeuvres we have found.

30 small brussel sprouts
3 oz. cream cheese
1 tbsp. whipped cream
1 1/2 tbsps. freshly grated horseradish
salt

Cook brussel sprouts for about 3 minutes in boiling,
salted water, only long enough to obtain a brilliant
green color. Be sure to remove from the fire before
they lose this color. Soften the cream cheese and mix
with the whipped cream. Add the horseradish. Cut
each brussel sprout 3/4 of the way through the center
and stuff with cheese mixture. Sprinkle the sprouts with
salt and let stand at room temperature for about 30
minutes before serving.

Viennese ham pockets

Your calorie-conscious friends will
abandon their diets for these.

PASTRY:
1 cup sifted flour
1/4 tsp. salt
1/4 lb. butter

3 oz. cream cheese
1 egg yolk

Sift the already sifted flour together with the salt onto a pastry board. Make a well in the center of the flour and add remaining ingredients. With fingers, work ingredients into flour until dough is smooth. Chill for at least 1 hour.

FILLING:
1 cup finely chopped ham
1 small onion, finely chopped
1 tbsp. chopped parsley

1 tsp. Dijon mustard
1/4 tsp. pepper
1 tbsp. sweet pickle relish

Combine all ingredients. Roll out pastry onto lightly floured board until very thin. Cut into 2-inch squares. Place 1 teaspoon of filling in the center of each square. Pull the four corners to center and pinch edges to seal. Chill filled squares for about 1 hour. Bake filled squares ▶

LIVER STRUDEL

These are so flaky and delicate no one will guess they are so easy to prepare.

3 oz. cream cheese
1/3 cup butter
2/3 cup flour

1 unbeaten egg white
2 small cans liver pâté

Place cream cheese, butter, and flour into a bowl and mix thoroughly with fingers until ingredients are well blended and dough is smooth. Chill. Roll out onto a lightly floured board until thin. Cut into 2-inch squares. Form liver pâté into a pencil shape about 2-inches long, then place along one edge of each square. Roll each up and seal with unbeaten white of egg. (Or place unsealed rolls on baking pan with the flap on bottom.) Bake on ungreased pan for about 15 minutes in 450° oven, or until golden.

Makes about 30 squares.

✦ ✦ ✦

on ungreased pan in hot oven (450°) for about 10 minutes until they are golden. Serve hot.

It is preferable to make these in advance and bake when needed, or they may be baked and reheated. They may be frozen baked or unbaked.

Makes approximately 36 pockets.

VIENNESE *sardellen* SHELLS

In Vienna, these are often baked in scallop shells and served as a first course.

1 2-oz. tin anchovies, drained
4 tbsps. butter
3 egg yolks
1/3 cup grated Parmesan cheese

1 tbsp. chopped parsley
3 egg whites, beaten stiff
toasted rounds of very thinly sliced bread

Mash anchovies into a pulp or pass through a sieve. Cream the butter and add egg yolks one at a time until thoroughly blended. Add anchovies, cheese, and parsley to egg and butter mixture. Blend thoroughly. Fold in egg whites. Pile onto toast rounds and bake in moderate (350°) oven for about 8 minutes, or until lightly browned.

These may be reheated later, but be careful not to get them too brown when first baking them.

Makes approximately 60 shells.

*The caraway seeds give this cheese
pastry an unusual flavor.*

*2 cups sifted flour
1 tsp. salt
2/3 cup shortening
4–5 tbsps. cold water*

*1 cup freshly grated Swiss
cheese
1 tbsp. caraway seeds*

Sift together the already sifted flour and the salt. Cut in shortening until mixture resembles small peas. Add water 1 tablespoon at a time until dough holds together. Do not handle too much. Chill. Divide dough into 2 parts. Roll it out, very thin, into rectangles. Sprinkle 1 part with cheese and top it with caraway seeds and a sprinkle of salt. Place other half of dough on top of this as a cover. Chill for 5 minutes in refrigerator. Cut filled dough into strips 2-inches long and 1/4-inch wide. Chill again before baking. Place on ungreased cookie sheet and bake in hot oven (450°) for about 5 minutes, or until golden.

These may be prepared for baking several days in advance and kept in the refrigerator, or they may be baked and kept in a covered container for about 1 week. Reheat in a slow oven before serving.

Makes about 7-dozen sticks.

Fondue

There are those who think it heresy to drink anything but kirsch with Fondue, but don't let this stop you. As someone said, "Perfect for the guest who hates to stop drinking to eat."

1 lb. Swiss cheese, coarsely grated
3 tbsps. flour
2 cups dry white wine
2 cloves garlic
3-4 tbsps. kirsch or cognac
1/4 tsp. salt
dash of nutmeg
bite-size pieces of French bread

Pour 2 cups dry white wine into chafing dish or heavy skillet. Put garlic through a press and add to the wine. Cook over low heat until tiny bubbles rise to the surface. *Do not allow to boil.* Turn heat very low and add cheese, coated with flour, a handful at a time, stirring constantly. Be sure each addition of cheese is completely melted before adding more. Keep stirring until mixture starts to bubble, then season with salt and a dash of nutmeg. Add kirsch or cognac. Continue stirring until mixture bubbles gently again. Each guest then spears a piece of French bread, with crust on, with a fork and dunks it into the Fondue, swirling the fork as he dips.

This recipe serves 4 famished people, but as an hors d'oeuvre it should keep 12 people happy for a while.

A novel way to treat olives—and
we highly recommend it.

1 9-oz. can green olives, with pits
1/2 cup vinegar
1/4 cup salad oil
1 green chili pepper, chopped
1 clove garlic, minced
1 tsp. oregano

Put olives, with juice from can, into large jar or bowl. Add remaining ingredients and marinate for several days. Serve cold.

These will keep for several weeks in the refrigerator.

Makes approximately 55 olives.

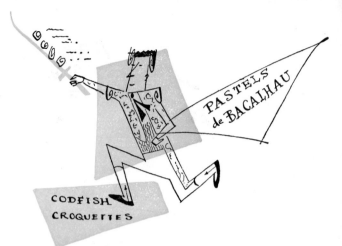

CODFISH CROQUETTES

PASTELS de BACALHAU

Codfish is to Portugal what baked beans are to Boston.

1 cup flaked salt codfish	1 tsp. melted butter
2 cups pared and diced raw potatoes	few grains pepper
	1 tsp. salt (optional)
1 egg, slightly beaten	1/4 tsp. celery salt
1/4 tsp. paprika	2 cups water

If dried codfish is used, soak fish overnight, changing water several times. Flake the fish. (You may buy flaked codfish in the can in some areas.) Cook fish and potatoes in a covered pan with about 2 cups of boiling water until well done. Drain well. Mash thoroughly. Add egg, paprika, melted butter, celery salt, and pepper. Add a little salt, if desired. Beat until light and fluffy. Chill. Form mixture into small balls about the size of a walnut. Fry in deep fat until golden brown. Serve on picks with a bowl of chili sauce and a bowl of pickles.

Codfish croquettes may be prepared several days in advance and refrigerated, or frozen and reheated in a hot oven (450°) before serving.

Makes about 60 croquettes.

EGGPLANT MARINARA

This recipe is quite different from the ordinary fare. It is colorful and usually a conversation piece.

> 1 eggplant, peeled and
>   cut into 1-inch cubes
> 1/4 cup wine vinegar
> 1/4 tsp. basil
> 1/4 tsp. oregano
> 1/4 tsp. salt
> 1/8 tsp. pepper
> 1 clove garlic, minced
> 2 tbsps. olive oil

Cook eggplant cubes in boiling, salted water until tender but not too soft, about 3 minutes. Combine remaining ingredients, except olive oil, and marinate cooked eggplant in vinegar-seasoning mixture overnight in refrigerator. Just before serving add olive oil. Serve on picks.

Makes approximately 60 cubes.

ITALY 27

Baby Pizza

These are so popular you might want to double the recipe.

1 package Hot Roll Mix (or use your favorite Italian bread recipe)
1 large onion, chopped
1 1/2 cloves garlic, minced
1 1/2 tbsps. olive oil
6 oz. tomato sauce
2 tbsps. water
1/4 tsp. celery salt
1/4 tsp. oregano
1/4 tsp. rosemary
salt and pepper to taste
dash of Accent (msg)
1/2 lb. Mozzarella cheese
1/4 lb. pepperoni
1/4 cup grated Parmesan cheese

Follow directions on box of Hot Roll Mix and let dough rise once. Sauté onions and garlic in the olive oil until golden. Add tomato sauce, water, and seasonings. Let this simmer while dough is rising. When dough has doubled in size, take a small piece, about the size of a marble, put it onto an ungreased cookie sheet, and pat into a circle about 1 1/2 inches in diameter. (A little oil on the fingers makes it easier to stretch dough to proper size and to handle it.) Make sure dough is thin. On each circle, spoon about 1 teaspoonful of sauce. Top with thin slice of Mozzarella ▶

marinated **Anchovies**

_Anchovies are always successful as hors d'oeuvres.
This recipe is no exception, but the flavor
is a pleasant surprise._

2 cans rolled anchovy filets with capers
2 tbsps. red-wine vinegar
2 tsps. grated onion
1 tsp. chopped parsley
1/2 clove garlic, minced

Place anchovies and oil from can in a shallow dish.
Add remaining ingredients and marinate at least 1 hour,
but preferably longer. Serve with picks.

Makes approximately 26 small hors d'oeuvres.

✦ ✦ ✦

▶ cheese and a slice of pepperoni. Sprinkle with grated
Parmesan cheese.   Bake for 7 to 10 minutes in hot oven
(450°) until cheese is bubbly and crust begins to brown.
Serve hot!

These may be refrigerated and reheated or they may
be frozen baked or unbaked.

Makes 36 bite-size pizza.

Marinated Mushrooms

*No matter how many times we doubled this
recipe there were never any left over.*

1 lb. fresh button mushrooms
1/4 cup olive oil
1/2 cup wine vinegar
1/2 onion, grated or finely chopped
1 clove garlic, minced

If mushrooms are very small, leave stems on; if large,
remove stems and save for some other dish. Cook
mushrooms in boiling, salted water for 10 minutes.
Drain well. Make a French dressing with remaining
ingredients and marinate mushrooms for at least 12
hours. Serve on picks.

Makes about 30 mushrooms.

Prosciutto e Melone

*These are excellent summer hors d'oeuvres—
refreshing and low in calorie content.*

1 honeydew melon
1/2 lb. Prosciutto (*Italian raw smoked ham*)

Cut melon into 1-inch cubes. Wrap each cube in a piece of ham. (If Italian ham is not available, dried beef may be used instead.) Serve on picks.

If melon is not too ripe, hors d'oeuvres may be made about 1 hour in advance and refrigerated.

Makes approximately 100 cubes.

The pizza lover will enjoy these,
and they are easy to make

1 tin anchovy fillets
1/4 lb. Mozzarella cheese, thinly sliced
1/2 tsp. oregano
30 thin toast rounds, about 1 1/2 inches in diameter

Place thin slice (about 1/8-inch thick) of Mozzarella cheese on a round of toast. Cut anchovy fillets in half. Place both halves on top of cheese. Sprinkle with a few pieces of dried oregano. Put under a moderate broiler for 1 or 2 minutes until the cheese melts.

These may be prepared for broiling in advance, but they should be served as soon as possible after they have been broiled.

Makes 30 Spiedini.

KEPTETHES

(BAKED MEAT BALLS)

The cinnamon and mint combine to give these an interesting flavor.

1 lb. ground beef	1/2 tsp. salt
2 medium onions, chopped finely	1/8 tsp. pepper
1 cup bread crumbs	1 #2-can tomatoes
1 cup water	1/2 tsp. cinnamon
1 tbsp. dried mint leaf	1/4 cup butter

Combine meat, onions, mint leaf, bread crumbs, water, salt, and pepper in a large bowl and mix well. Shape mixture into small egg-shaped balls. Place balls in a baking dish. Strain tomatoes through a sieve and pour over meat balls. Dot each ball with a piece of butter and sprinkle with cinnamon. Bake in 400° oven for 1 hour, or until nicely browned. Turn at least once to brown evenly.

These can be made in advance and refrigerated or frozen to be reheated when needed.

Makes approximately 80 meat balls.

Stuffed Cabbage
with sweet and sour sauce

The beauty of this recipe is that the flavor improves if it is made a day or more in advance.

1 lb. ground beef
1 egg, beaten
1/2 onion, grated
1/4 cup rice, uncooked
salt and pepper
2 heads cabbage

1 8-oz. can tomato sauce
2 onions, sliced
3 tbsps. butter
1/2 cup brown sugar
2 lemons, juice of
1 bay leaf

Boil cabbage until tender but not soft (about 5 minutes) in salted water. Mix meat, rice, egg, grated onion, salt, and pepper. Cut cabbage leaves into 4-inch squares and fill each square with 1 teaspoon of meat mixture. Melt butter in deep skillet. Add sliced onions and sauté until golden. Place cabbage balls into skillet. Sprinkle with brown sugar and lemon juice. Add tomato sauce and bay leaf. Bake until brown in 350° oven, uncovered, for about 1 hour.

These may be refrigerated and reheated a day or so later and are actually better this way.

The stuffing is also delicious when made into very small meat balls and served on toothpicks.

Makes approximately 80.

*The flavors blend together better if allowed
to "meld" for a day or so.*

> 1/4 lb. cream cheese
> 3 tbsps. chopped chives
> 1 1/2 tbsps. lime juice
> 1 tbsp. chopped parsley
> 1 can Norwegian sardines
> 1/8 tsp. salt

Cream the cheese with lime juice until it is smooth. Add remaining ingredients and mix until well blended. Fill Puff Shells (page 16) or serve on celery or as a dip.

This cream may be kept in refrigerator for about a week or it can be frozen. Filled Puff shells may also be frozen.

Makes about one cup or enough for 40 Puff Shells.

ANCHOYY STUFFED EGGS

In Sweden these would be one small part of an extensive array of predinner food—smorgasbord.

> **12 hard-cooked eggs**
> **4 tbsps. anchovy paste**
> **1/4 cup mayonnaise**
> **2 tsps. sugar**
> **2 tbsps. finely chopped parsley**

Cut eggs in half lengthwise and remove yolks. Mash yolks with silver fork. Add anchovy paste, mayonnaise, and sugar and blend well. Fill egg whites with mixture and sprinkle with finely chopped parsley.

Makes 24 hors d'oeuvres.

Swedish meat-ball recipes vary from household to household. We think this one is especially good.

3/4 lb. beef, ground	*2 tsps. salt*
1/4 lb. lean pork, ground	*1/2 tsp. pepper*
1/4 lb. veal, ground	*2 tbsps. minced onion*
1/2 cup milk	*2 eggs*
1/2 cup bread crumbs	*3 tbsps. butter, or more*

Have butcher grind meat together twice. Sauté onions in about $1/2$ teaspoonful of butter unti soft, but not brown. Beat eggs and milk together and pour over bread crumbs. When mixture is soft add it to meat and work well together. Add spices and onion and blend all together until light and fluffy. Form into balls about the size of a walnut. Brown in remaining butter, a few at a time. Keep turning balls so they retain their shape and brown evenly. Add more butter, if necessary.

These may be made 1 or 2 days in advance and reheated, or they may be frozen and reheated.

Makes approximately 70 balls.

SWEDEN 37

Danish MEAT BALLS

This recipe received "Honorable Mention" in the International Cooking Contest in Tokyo. The sausage makes them divine.

1 lb. ground beef
1/2 lb. sausage
1/2 cup flour
1 doz. Ritz-type crackers, finely crushed (or 1 cup flour)
1 cup sweet cream
2 eggs, beaten
2 tbsps. chopped onion
1 tbsp. (scant) salt
1 tsp. pepper
1 tsp. sugar

Mix beef, sausage, flour, and crushed crackers well. Add remaining ingredients. Chill. Form into balls about the size of a walnut. Fry in butter or margarine.

These may be refrigerated or frozen before or after frying.

Makes approximately 50 small balls.

Piroshky

These egg-shaped specialties are filled with a well-flavored meat and encased in a yeast dough.

DOUGH:

1 cup quite warm water	1 tsp. salt
1 cup milk	1/4 lb. butter
3 egg yolks	4 cups all-purpose flour
3 tbsps. sugar	1 package yeast

Dissolve yeast in the water. Heat milk and add the butter to melt. Beat egg yolks and add sugar and salt. Add milk and butter to egg mixture, then add yeast mixture and stir. Sift flour and add it to make a dough. The dough will be somewhat thin. Cover and put in a warm place. Let it rise for 1 to 1 1/2 hours.

FILLING:

1 lb. ground beef	1 tbsp. salt
4 medium onions, chopped	1/4 tsp. pepper
3 hard-cooked eggs, chopped	

Cook onions in butter until soft. Add meat, salt, and pepper and cook until meat is done. Add chopped hard-cooked eggs and cool.

Add enough flour to dough to enable you to roll it ▶

PIROSHKY (cont.)

▶ out on a *very-well-floured* board. Be sure to keep hands *well floured* at all times. It helps to do a small portion at a time and knead with flour before rolling out. Roll to approximately 1/8-inch thickness and cut into 1 1/2-inch circles. Place 1/2 teaspoon of filling on each circle and stretch dough up to the center. Pinch outer rim together. Filled pocket should resemble a tapered egg. Fry each pocket in deep fat until golden brown.

These may be made in advance and reheated or they may be frozen either deep-fried or not.

Makes approximately 100 small Piroshky.

Cairo Meat Pies

Good for a large party.   Very inexpensive.

DOUGH:

3 cups flour
1 cup water
1/2 tsp. salt

Add the water to the flour and salt and mix well. Knead until smooth. Chill.

FILLING:

1 lb. lean beef, ground
2 oz. beef suet, minced
1/8 tsp. allspice
1/8 tsp. pepper
1/2 tsp. salt
1/4 tsp. cinnamon

4 tbsps. oil
1 6-oz. can tomato paste
1 tsp. chopped parsley
3 small onions, chopped
5 tbsps. lemon juice
1 cup coarsely chopped walnuts

Combine all ingredients and mix well.

Roll out dough on a well-floured board until very thin. Cut rolled dough into 1 1/2-inch circles. Place 1 teaspoon of filling on each circle. Fold in half and seal edge. Fry in deep fat until golden.

These pies may be frozen and fried when needed.

Makes approximately 200 tiny pies.

Gefulte Fish

*Traditionally served as a first course
on Friday night (Sabbath eve).*

3 lbs. carp (or mixture of
  carp, pike, and rockfish)
4 medium onions
2 carrots
2 stalks celery
few sprigs parsley
1 egg
1/3 cup water
1 tbsp. matzo meal or fine
  cracker crumbs
1 tbsp. salt
1 tsp. sugar
1/2 tsp. pepper

Fillet and salt the fish and refrigerate overnight. Save skin and bones. In the bottom of a 4-quart pot, place skin and bones of fish; 2 onions, sliced; 2 carrots, sliced; the celery and parsley; and 1 quart of cold water. Bring this to a boil and let simmer for 10 minutes.

Put filleted fish and 2 onions through finest blade of meat grinder at least twice. Add 1/3 cup of water, the egg, matzo meal, salt, sugar, and 1/4 teaspoon of pepper. Mix ingredients together well. Wet palms of hands and form balls about the size of walnuts. Place balls carefully into boiling water. Add remaining pepper and more salt, if necessary. Be sure water covers balls. Simmer for about 2 hours. Chill. Serve on toothpicks.

Carrots make a pretty garnish. These are usually served with grated horseradish, which is flavored with beets.

Makes approximately 100 balls.

The proportions of these ingredients vary from cook to cook. And there are those who wouldn't dream of frying the onions. We like this recipe.

> **1 lb. chicken livers**
> **5 medium onions, chopped**
> **4 hard-cooked eggs**
> **1/4 cup chicken fat**
> **salt and pepper to taste**

Sauté onions in chicken fat. Flavor is improved if a few of the onions turn black. Add chicken livers and cook until done (about 5 minutes). Put mixture, together with the hard-cooked eggs, through meat grinder or food mill (or chop as finely as you can). Chill. Serve with rye or black bread or on crackers.

This will keep a few days, or it may be frozen. However, after thawing, use immediately.

Makes approximately 3 cups.

If you haven't tried grape leaves fixed in this fashion, you've missed a real treat.

1/2 lb. ground beef	1/4 tsp. pepper
1/2 cup rice, uncooked	grape leaves (preferably
1 tsp. salt	young pale green ones)

Boil leaves in salt water for 5 minutes. Drain. Mix meat, rice, salt, and pepper. Roll about 1 teaspoonful of meat mixture in grape leaves diagonally. Keep in mind that rice will swell. Place filled leaves together in bundles of 8 or 10 and tie loosely with white thread. Put a few grape leaves in bottom of pan to prevent scorching. Place bundles of stuffed leaves on top of the loose leaves. Cover with water. Drop in a cut clove of garlic. Cook gently over low heat until water is absorbed (about 1/2 to 3/4 of an hour). Serve hot with toothpicks.

These may be prepared in advance and reheated.

Makes about 40 Yabra.

BEUREKS

Our Turkish expert says true Beureks are only made with Feta cheese, but these are delicious with Gruyère cheese nevertheless.

pie dough for two-crust pie
1/2 lb. Feta cheese (or Gruyère cheese if Feta is not available)

1 tbsp. butter
1 1/2 tbsps. flour
1/4 cup milk
salt and pepper to taste

Make a thick cream sauce with butter, flour, and milk. Cut cheese into small pieces and add to cream sauce, cooking until cheese melts and mixture thickens. Pour mixture onto a platter to cool. Chill. Form into small sausage shapes. Roll out pie dough very thin. Cut into 2-inch squares. Place cheese sausages in the middle of the squares and fold squares to make triangles. Deep-fry in very hot fat. Serve hot or cold.

These can be prepared in advance and fried when needed, or they may be fried and reheated. They may also be frozen.

Makes about 36 Beureks.

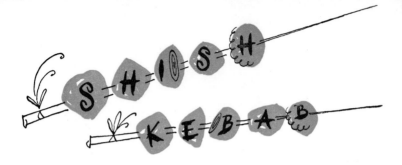

*Try these on the outdoor grill.
Men really go for them.*

1 lb. lean lamb, cut into 1-inch cubes
1/4 cup olive oil
6 tbsps. sherry
1 tsp. salt
2 small, firm tomatoes, cut into wedges
1 large onion, cut into thick slices
1 large green pepper, cut into small squares
1 lb. whole mushrooms
1/4 tsp. pepper
1 clove garlic, minced
1 tsp. oregano

Combine oil, sherry, salt, pepper, oregano, and garlic. Marinate lamb several hours or overnight in refrigerator. Turn occasionally. Place 1 cube meat, 1 wedge tomato, 2 pieces onion, 1 piece green pepper, and 1 mushroom cap (remove stems and use for something else) on a skewer. Broil slowly for about 15 minutes. Turn frequently and baste with marinade while broiling.

Makes about 40 hearty Kebabs.

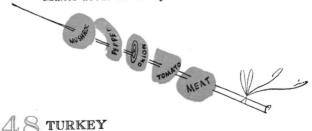

If you're tired of canned nuts, try these; they are truly exotic.

1/4 cup salad oil
1 tbsp. curry powder
1 tbsp. Worcestershire sauce
1 tbsp. chutney, put through a fine sieve
dash cayenne
1/2 lb. shelled walnuts

Heat oil in skillet and add remaining seasonings, heating thoroughly. Add walnuts and stir until well coated. Spread them on cooking sheet lined with brown paper and bake in 300° oven for about 10 minutes, until crisp.

These may be made in advance and reheated or first frozen and then reheated.

Yields about 2 1/2 cups of walnut halves.

CURRIED CHICKEN BALLS

Try this with leftover chicken or canned chicken.

1/2 cup cooked chicken
1/2 tsp. curry powder
1 1/2 tsps. chutney syrup
salt and pepper to taste
1/4 cup chopped parsley

Put chicken through finest blade of a grinder. Moisten with chutney syrup to form a paste. Add curry powder, salt, and pepper. Form mixture into small balls about the size of marbles. Roll in finely chopped parsley. Chill. Serve on toothpicks.

These may be refrigerated or frozen.

Makes about 26 balls.

Now here's something to do with that little piece of leftover lamb.

> *1 cup lamb, cooked, ground*
> *2 tbsps. chutney*
> *1/2 tsp. curry powder*
> *1/2 tsp. prepared mustard*
> *1 tbsp. butter*
> *1/4 cup shaved almonds*

To ground meat, add remaining ingredients, except nuts. Form into balls the size of large marbles. Roll in shaved almonds. Chill. Serve on toothpicks.

These may be refrigerated or frozen.

Makes about 40 balls.

NOTE

All measurements of soy sauce refer to Japanese *shoyu*. If you are unable to obtain the Japanese variety, reduce the quantity by half or dilute the soy sauce with an equal amount of water. American soy sauce is more highly concentrated and saltier than the Japanese variety.

CRAB BALLS

This is the specialty of one of our favorite Japanese cooks.

1 6 1/2-oz. can crabmeat
1 tbsp. butter
1 tbsp. flour
1/2 cup milk
1/2 tsp. salt
1/2 cup cornstarch

Melt the butter. Add flour until mixture is thick then add milk slowly to make a thick cream sauce. Bring to a boil and add crabmeat and salt. Chill. Form into balls the size of a walnut. Roll in cornstarch. Deep-fry. Serve hot with soy sauce and hot mustard.

Crab balls may be prepared an hour or so in advance and reheated in hot oven (450°).

Makes about 30 balls.

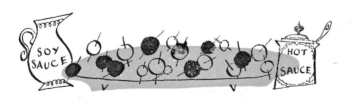

LOTUS ROOT BALLS

*Although similar in taste to fried oysters, these
lotus balls are more delicate in texture*

1/2 cup grated lotus root*
1/4 tsp. salt
1 tbsp. flour

Mix above ingredients together and form balls about the size of a walnut. Deep-fry and serve on picks.

Another attractive addition to the hors d'oeuvre tray is sliced lotus root, deep-fried and salted. It resembles a lace doily in appearance.

Makes about 25 balls.

* If lotus root is not available, try raw sweet potato as a substitute.

PICKLED TURNIPS

The very appearance of these attractive hors d'oeuvres will make your snack tray a success. Incidentally, they are delicious.

1/2 lb. small turnips
3 tbsps. vinegar
2 tbsps. mirin (or sweet sherry)
1/2 tsp. salt
red caviar

Marinate turnips in vinegar, mirin, and salt for, at least half an hour. Remove from marinade. Slice each turnip from the top into quarters or eighths, being careful not to cut all the way through. Decorate top of each with red caviar.

Makes approximately 8 to 10 turnips.

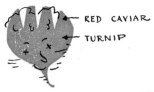

RED CAVIAR

TURNIP

Salmon snappers

Snappers are an inexpensive but elegant dish.

1 6 1/2-oz. can salmon, drained
3 tbsps. minced onion
1/2 tsp. salt
1/4 tsp. pepper
1 egg yolk
10 slices day-old bread

Remove crusts from bread and cut each slice into 6 parts. With a sharp knife, cut each square as though slicing it again, but do not slice all the way through. Mix remaining ingredients until well blended. Place a scant teaspoonful of salmon mixture inside each cut square, like a sandwich. Fry in deep fat until golden brown. Drain on absorbent paper.

These snappers may be prepared in advance and fried when needed or they may be prefried and reheated when needed. They may be frozen either before frying or after. And, as a matter of fact, they need not be very hot when served, and can be prepared an hour in advance.

Makes approximately 60 snappers.

Tempura

Tempura may be made from many things other than shrimp. It is common in Japan to tempura vegetables such as carrots, mushrooms, onions, scallions, etc., in the identical manner.

2 lbs. prawns or large shrimp
1 cup water
1 egg
1 cup all-purpose flour
soy sauce (*see p. 54*)

Shell and de-vein large shrimp or prawns, leaving tail attached to flesh. Slit undersection of shrimp to prevent curling. Wash and dry thoroughly. Prepare batter by beating egg and water together, then adding flour and mixing lightly. Two or three stirs should be enough, even though some lumps may remain. Dip shrimp into batter, holding them by tails, and deep-fry in hot oil for just a few minutes. Serve with soy sauce, if possible.

Approximately 30 servings.

TERIYAKI

In Japan, if fish is not served raw, it is usually prepared in this fashion.

1 lb. fish (*salmon, tuna, rock-fish, or mackerel*), *filleted*
3/4 cup soy sauce (*see p. 54*)
1/4 cup sugar
3/4 cup mirin (*or sweet sherry*)

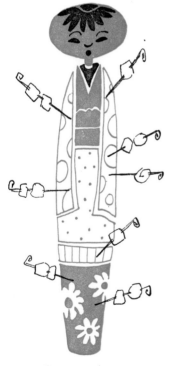

Cut fillets into small pieces (about 1-inch square). Mix remaining ingredients and marinate fish squares for about 30 minutes. Place 1 or 2 on bamboo or metal skewers and broil until done. Serve hot. The flavor is improved if these are broiled over charcoal.

Makes approximately 40 squares of fish.

Yakitori is instantly popular with people tasting it for the first time. In Japan, it is always broiled over charcoal.

1/2 lb. raw white chicken meat, cut into bite-size pieces
1/4 lb. chicken livers
5 stalks large scallions, cut into 1 1/2-inch strips
8 tsps. mirin (or sweet sherry)
1 cup soy sauce (see p. 54)
2 tbsps. sugar

Cook mirin, soy sauce, and sugar over low heat for 10–15 minutes, until mixture thickens slightly. Skewer meat and/or livers and scallions on 5-inch bamboo picks and broil until done. Pour sauce over meat and put skewers back under broiler for 1 minute. For sure-fire success, let each guest broil his own hors d'oeuvres, when you are cooking outside on a charcoal grill.

Makes approximately 30 servings.

CH'IAO TZU

PASTRY:
1 1/2 cups sifted enriched flour
5–6 tbsps. cold water

Make a stiff dough. Add more water, if necessary. Knead thoroughly to make dough smooth and roll out to 3/4-inch thickness. Cut rolled dough into 1/2-inch squares. Flatten these and roll them out onto floured board to rounds about 2 inches in diameter. The rounds should be thin. Sprinkle each round with cornstarch and stack until ready to use.

FILLING:
1 package frozen spinach, parboiled, drained until dry, and finely chopped
1/2 lb. pork, finely chopped
1 tsp. finely chopped fresh ginger (or substitute 1/8 tsp. powdered ginger)
1/2 onion, finely chopped
1/2 tbsp. oil
1 tbsp. sesame, peanut, or salad oil
1 1/2 tbsps. soy sauce (see p. 54)
1 1/2 tsps. salt

Sauté the onion, ginger, and pork in the oil until pork is thoroughly cooked. It will be white in color. Add sesame oil, soy sauce, and salt. When mixture cools, add spinach.

Put a teaspoonful of meat mixture on rolled-out ▶

Chinese MEAT BALLS

This is not just another meat ball. The crunchy texture makes it quite unusual.

2 eggs
1 tbsp. soy sauce *(see p. 54)*
1 tsp. sugar
1 tsp. salt
1/4 tsp. msg. *(Accent, Aji-no-moto)*
1 lb. lean pork, ground
3/4 cup chopped scallions
1/2 cup chopped Chinese cabbage, *(substitute regular cabbage if Chinese variety is not available)*
1/4 cup flour

Beat eggs and add soy sauce and sugar. Add meat, scallions, and cabbage and mix until well blended. Add salt, msg., and flour and knead well. Form into balls the size of a walnut. Fry in hot oil about 1-inch deep. Drain on paper towels. Serve on toothpicks.

These may be made in advance, refrigerated or frozen, and reheated.

Makes 60 meat balls.

▶pastry. Fold over to make a semicircle. Pinch the edges together. Deep-fry. Serve hot!

These may be made in advance and frozen, cooked or uncooked.

Makes approximately 30 dumplings.

Shrimp toast

This is one of our favorites, and we guarantee its popularity.

1 lb. shrimp, uncooked
2 tbsps. minced fresh ginger, (or 1/4 tsp. ground ginger)
1/2 cup finely chopped onion
1 tsp. salt
1/8 tsp. pepper

2 egg whites, slightly beaten
1/4 cup fine bread crumbs or cracker meal
approximately 15 slices stale bread

Shell and de-vein shrimp and chop to a fine consistency. Add onion, ginger, salt, and pepper and bind together with egg white.

Cut bread into rounds or squares of approximately 1 inch. Spread bread slices with shrimp paste and dredge tops with bread crumbs. Fry in deep fat until golden brown.

These may be made in advance, refrigerated for one day or frozen, and deep-fried when needed.

Makes approximately 75 pieces.

*These have a more delicate flavor than most
sweet and sour spareribs.*

2 lbs. meaty spareribs
1/4 cup soy sauce (*see p. 54*)
1/2 cup sugar
1/2 cup vinegar
1/4 cup sherry
1 tbsp. soy sauce

1/2 tbsp. cornstarch
1 tbsp. water
1 tbsp. chopped fresh ginger
 (or 1/8 tsp. powdered ginger)

Have butcher cut spareribs into individual bite-size
pieces. Brush them with 1/4-cup soy sauce and bake in
moderate oven (350°) for about 1 hour, or until they are
brown and crisp.

Bring to a boil the sugar, vinegar, sherry, and the
tablespoon of soy sauce. Add the cornstarch which has
been mixed with water and stir until transparent. Add
ginger. Pour over spareribs and serve hot.

Spareribs may be made in advance, refrigerated or
frozen, and reheated.

Makes about 40 servings.

$\mathcal{S}$PRING ROLLS

Make these on a rainy day when you have lots of time. Don't let your family eat them all before the guests have a chance.

WRAPPINGS:

1 1/2 cups water   2 cups flour

Add the flour to the water slowly, stirring until batter is smooth and thin. Heat a lightly greased skillet over a moderate flame and pour in 1 tablespoon of batter, tilting the skillet to spread batter as thinly as possible. (You may brush batter on with a pastry brush, if the pan is not too hot.) Wrapping should be about 4 inches in diameter. Heat for about 1 minute, just long enough to set on one side only. Remove wrapping from pan and make the next one. Do not stack wrappings until they are cool. Be sure to sprinkle cornstarch between them so they will not stick to each other. You may refrigerate wrappings so stacked or freeze them for later use.

FILLING:

2 cups finely diced bamboo shoots

3 cups fresh bean sprouts (or 1 1/2 cups canned bean sprouts, well drained)

3 tbsps. soy sauce (see p. 54)

1 tbsp. sherry

1 tbsp. finely chopped fresh ginger (or 1/8 tsp. powdered ginger)

1/2 cup dried mushrooms

1/2 lb. lean pork, ground

1/2 lb. raw shrimp, chopped

2 tbsps. chopped scallions

3 tbsps. oil

1 tsp. cornstarch

1 tsp. salt

1 tbsp. cornstarch

1/2 cup water

Soak dried mushrooms in lukewarm water for 15 to 20 minutes, until they are soft. Drain. Remove stems. (They are too tough to eat.) Chop caps finely.

Sauté bamboo shoots in 1 tablespoon of oil. Add bean sprouts and heat thoroughly. Add 2 tablespoons of soy sauce and continue to heat for a minute longer. Remove from pan to large bowl.

Reheat pan and add 1 tablespoon of oil. Sauté chopped scallions and chopped mushrooms. Remove them from pan and add to mixture in bowl.

Combine 1 tablespoon of soy sauce, 1 tablespoon of sherry, 1 teaspoon of cornstarch, and 1 teaspoon of salt. Dredge pork and shrimp with this mixture.

Reheat pan and add 1 tablespoon of oil. Sauté seasoned meat until pork is well cooked. Add ginger and combine all ingredients. Mix well.

Place about 1 1/2 teaspoons of filling on each wrapping. Roll up, tucking in ends, and seal with a mixture of cornstarch and water.

Fry in deep, hot fat. Serve with soy sauce and hot mustard.

These hors d'oeuvres may be made in advance and refrigerated or frozen. They may be stored before or after frying. If before frying, sprinkle with cornstarch and wrap in wax paper also sprinkled with cornstarch to prevent sticking. If stored after frying, reheat in very hot oven so they become crisp.

Makes approximately 50 cocktail-size Spring Rolls.

ADOBO

Adobo is a national dish in the Philippines and is often served as a main course.

1/2 lb. raw chicken meat, cut in small pieces
1/4 lb. raw lean pork, cut in 1-inch cubes
1/4 lb. chicken livers

1/4 cup vinegar
1 tbsp. water
1/2 tsp. salt
1/8 tsp. pepper
2 cloves garlic, crushed

Combine vinegar, water, salt, pepper, and garlic. Marinate meat in mixture for an hour. Remove livers. Drain them. Bring liquid to a boil and cook chicken and pork until tender. Drain these too. Deep-fry the chicken, pork, and chicken livers until crisp and brown. (Adobo has a strong odor while cooking, so it is better to prepare in advance and to deep-fry just before serving, or deep-fry early and reheat it.) Serve on picks.

Makes about 30 servings.

LUMPIA

WRAPPINGS:
2 cups flour
1 1/2 cups water

Mix ingredients together to form thin batter. Lightly grease a small skillet. Pour about a tablespoon of batter on skillet and tilt so the batter spreads as thinly as possible. Each tablespoon should make a round of about 4 inches in diameter. (If the pan is not hot, you may brush the batter on with a pastry brush.) Remove each wrapping from pan and continue with the next. (See recipe for Spring Rolls, page 66.)

FILLING:

1/2 lb. lean pork, finely chopped	*1/8 tsp. pepper*
1/2 lb. fresh shrimp, finely chopped	*1 egg yolk*
1/2 cup mushrooms, finely chopped	*1 tbsp. soy sauce*
1/4 cup water chestnuts, chopped	*(see p. 54)*
2 tbsps. chives, chopped	*1 tbsp. cornstarch*
1/2 tsp. salt	*1/2 cup water*

Mix all ingredients together so they are well blended. Place about 1 teaspoonful on each wrapping. Fold the edges in and roll. Seal with mixture of 1 tablespoon of cornstarch and 1/2 cup of water. Deep-fry.

These may be prefried and reheated in hot oven (400°).

Makes about 50 Lumpia.

Curried shrimps

*In Malaya Curried Shrimp is frequently
made with coconut milk.*

1/2 lb. cooked shrimp
3 tbsps. butter
1/2 onion, minced
1/2 apple, pared and minced
2 tsps. curry powder
1/4 tsp. mace
1/2 tsp. salt
2 tbsps. flour
2/3 cup milk
pinch of chili powder

Sauté onion and apple in the butter until soft. Add curry powder, mace, salt, chili powder, and flour. When mixture is pasty, add milk and cook until it thickens. Add shrimp. Spread mixture on crackers or on small rounds of toasted bread and heat in 400° oven until very hot.

The mixture may be made a day in advance and refrigerated.

Makes approximately 36 canapés.

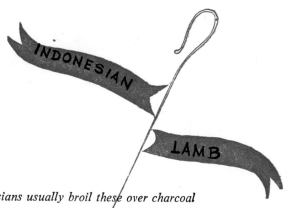

INDONESIAN LAMB

*Indonesians usually broil these over charcoal
and serve the meat with peanut sauce.*

   1 lb. lean lamb, cut in 1-inch cubes
   1/4 cup soy sauce (*see p. 54*)
   2 tbsps. lemon juice
   1 tsp. curry powder
   1 clove garlic, crushed

Mix soy sauce, lemon juice, curry powder, and garlic.
Marinate lamb in mixture for several hours or overnight
in refrigerator.   Turn occasionally.   Put 1 or 2 cubes of
meat on a skewer and broil 10 to 15 minutes, turning
once.

1 pound of meat makes about 40 1-inch cubes.

MINCED

SHRIMP BALLS

These shrimp balls are generally served in Indonesia as one of many accompaniments to rice.

2 cups cooked shrimp, minced
2 eggs, beaten
1 clove garlic, minced
1/4 cup bread crumbs
1/8 tsp. pepper
1/2 tsp. salt
dash nutmeg
1 tbsp. minced parsley

Mix all ingredients well. Form into balls about the size of large marbles. Deep-fry. (Mixture may be formed into small patties, about 1 1/2 inches in diameter, and fried in butter.) Either way, they may be frozen and reheated.

Makes approximately 24 patties.

Latin America

CHILI CHEESE BALLS

Attractive. Unusual. Delicious. Easy to make.

1/2 lb. cheddar cheese, grated
3 oz. cream cheese
1/2 clove garlic, crushed
1/4 cup chili powder

Combine cheddar cheese, cream cheese, and garlic until well blended. Make into small balls about the size of marbles. Roll these in chili powder and chill.

These may be kept in the refrigerator for about a week or they may be frozen.

Makes approximately 75 balls.

NACHOS

*Nachos are quite simple to make and
have a very distinctive flavor.*

1 can Mexican tortillas (18 to a can)
1/2 lb. sharp cheese, diced in to 1/2-inch cubes
1 small bottle pickled peppers

Cut tortillas into quarters. Place on baking sheet and
put into medium oven (350°) to toast. Remove from
oven before entirely crisped. Cut the cheese into 1/2-inch
cubes. Place 1 cube on each "tostado" and put them
back into oven until cheese melts. Garnish each with
a small slice of pickled pepper. Serve hot.

Makes about 72 Nachos.

GUACAMOLE

*There are as many recipes for Guacamole
as there are devotees of the dish.
This is our favorite.*

1 large ripe avocado
1/2 ripe tomato, peeled and
finely chopped
1/2 green pepper, seeded and
finely chopped
2 tsps. grated onion
1/2 tsp. chili powder
1/2 tsp. olive oil
1 tsp. lime juice
salt and pepper to taste

Mash avocado with a silver fork.
Add remaining ingredients and blend
well. (To keep Guacamole from darken-
ing, spread a heavy layer of mayonnaise on top and cover tightly. Just before serving stir the mayonnaise into the
mixture.) Serve with tortillas or potato
chips.

Makes about 3/4 cup.

Something new to do with the ever-popular shrimp.

1 lb. medium shrimp, cooked   1 bay leaf
1 cup vinegar   1 onion, sliced
2 tbsps. water   2 tsps. salt
3 whole cloves   1 tsp. sugar
1/4 tsp. pepper

Combine in a saucepan all ingredients except shrimp. Bring to a boil. Pour mixture over shrimp which have been shelled and de-veined. Marinate for at least 12 hours in refrigerator. Drain. Serve on picks.

Makes approximately 18–20 shrimp.

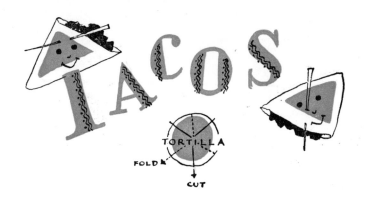

This is a mild version of a very
popular Mexican dish.

1 can tortillas (18 large tor-
   tillas)
1 onion, finely chopped
2 tbsps. butter
1/2 cup tomato juice

3 peeled green chilis, minced
1 cup shredded chicken
1/8 tsp. thyme
1 tsp. salt
dash cayenne

Sauté onion in the butter until golden. Add tomato
juice and chilis and mix well. Add remaining ingredients except tortillas and simmer for 3 minutes.

Place tortillas in hot fat for about 1 minute until they
are pliable. Remove from fat and drain. Cut into
thirds. Place 1 teaspoon of filling on each piece. Fold
each in half and secure with a toothpick. Heat until
crisp in 450° oven.

Tacos may be made in advance and popped into oven
when needed. Serve hot.

Makes approximately 54 Tacos.

*This delightful combination of ingredients
is exceedingly tempting to the palate.*

DOUGH :

2 cups flour, unsifted   1/4 cup lard
1/2 tsp. salt   1/2 cup milk, heated

Put flour on a board and make a hole in the center
of the flour. Melt lard in the heated milk. Add salt,
milk, and lard to the flour. Knead the dough with your
hands until it is well blended. Put in refrigerator overnight.

FILLING :

1/4 lb. beef, chopped   1/4 cup seedless raisins
1 large onion, chopped   2 tsps. cayenne
1 hard-cooked egg, sliced   1/2 tsp. salt
1/4 cup pitted ripe olives   2 tbsps. oil

Sauté beef in the oil. Add onions and cayenne and
brown them quickly. Remove dough from refrigerator.
Roll *very* thin. Cut half the dough into 1 1/2-inch circles
and the other half into 2-inch circles. Spread smaller
circles with 1/2 teaspoon of meat mixture. On top of
each, place 1/2 a pitted olive, 1/4 of one slice of egg, and
2 raisins. Put larger circles on top, wet edges with water,▶

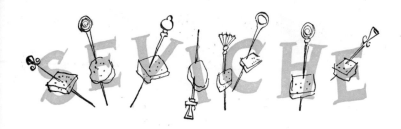

*You don't even have to cook this one—the
lime juice does it for you.*

> 1 cup raw scallops, cut in quarters
> 1/2 cup lime juice
> 2 tbsps. finely chopped onion
> 1 tbsp. finely chopped parsley
> 3 tbsps. olive oil
> 2 tbsps. finely chopped green pepper
> salt and pepper to taste

Cover scallops with the lime juice and marinate in refrigerator at least overnight. Drain. Add remaining ingredients and season to taste with salt and pepper. Serve in a bowl with picks handy.

Makes about 30 hors d'oeuvres.

▶and seal. Pinch edges with a fork. Brush with melted butter and bake in 425° oven for about 12 minutes, until golden.

These may be made in advance and baked when needed, or they may be frozen baked or unbaked. They are also delicious deep-fried.

Makes approximately 48 pies.

These alone are enough to make you want to go "South of the Border."

> 1 lb. raw shrimp
> 1 lemon, juice of
> 2 1/2 tbsps. oil
> 1 egg, well beaten
> 1/4 tsp. salt
> dash pepper
> 1/2 cup flour
> 1/4 cup warm water

Mix lemon juice and 2 tablespoons of the oil together. Add salt and pepper. Clean and de-vein shrimp. Marinate shrimp in lemon juice and oil for 30 minutes. Drain. Put 1 or 2 on a skewer. Make a thin batter with the flour, beaten egg, and remaining 1/2 tablespoon of oil. Add enough warm water to make batter thin. Dip skewered shrimp in batter and fry in deep, hot fat. Serve hot.

Makes about 20 servings.

CHEESE and BEEF DIP

The unusual feature of this dip is that it is served hot. It's nice for a chafing dish.

1/2 lb. sharp cheese, coarsely grated
1/4 lb. chipped beef, finely chopped
1 4-oz. can tomato sauce
1 clove garlic
1/2 beaten egg

Combine cheese, tomato sauce, beef, and garlic and heat over water in double boiler until cheese is melted. Remove garlic. Remove mixture from heat and add beaten egg. Age for several days in refrigerator. Reheat and serve as dip with crackers.

Makes about 3 cups.

UNITED STATES 85

CHEESE NUT BALL

African Porcupine

Your guests will start a guessing game about the contents of this surprising mixture.

> *1/4 lb. blue cheese*
> *3 oz. cream cheese*
> *1/4 lb. cheddar cheese (soft)*
> *1 onion, grated*
> *1 tsp. Worcestershire sauce*
> *1/4 lb. shelled pecans, coarsely chopped*
> *2 tbsps. chopped parsley*

Mix all ingredients except nuts and parsley with electric mixer until well blended. Add half the pecans. Form into large ball, wrap in waxed paper, and refrigerate overnight. Remove cheese ball from refrigerator about 1 hour before serving and roll in remaining nuts and chopped parsley, completely covering the outside. Serve with crackers surrounding the ball.

Makes about 1 1/2 cups; a ball about the size of a grapefruit.

cheese roll toast

These are good with beer or highballs, sherry or tea.

1 lb. cheddar cheese, grated
3 tbsps. mayonnaise
1 1/2 tbsps. prepared mustard
1/2 tsp. Worcestershire sauce
1/2 tsp. salt
1/2 tsp. paprika
20 thin slices of very fresh bread

Combine all ingredients except bread. Spread bread with the cheese mixture the same thickness as bread. Roll up like a jelly roll and wrap each roll in waxed paper and chill. Cut each roll into thirds. Just before serving, spread softened butter on rolls and broil until brown.

These can be frozen and reheated.

Makes approximately 60 rolls.

Chutney STUFFED Eggs

Crunchy. Slightly sweet. Delicious.

12 hard-cooked eggs
1/4 cup finely chopped chutney
6 slices crisp bacon
3 tbsps. mayonnaise

Cut eggs in half. Remove yolks and mash. Crumble bacon and add to mashed egg yolk together with chutney and mayonnaise. Fill whites, using a pastry tube for a pretty effect.

Makes 24 hors d'oeuvres.

CLAM PUFFS

If you like clams but are tired of the usual "dip," try this recipe.

3 oz. cream cheese
2 tbsps. heavy cream
1 7-oz. can minced clams, drained
    pinch dry mustard
    1/2 tsp. Worcestershire sauce
    1/4 tsp. salt
    1/2 tsp. grated onion
    paprika

Mix all of above ingredients together except paprika. Spread on toasted bread rounds or saltines and put in broiler for a few minutes until puffy. Sprinkle with paprika and serve piping hot!

This mixture may be made up a day or two ahead of time, spread on rounds and popped under the broiler at the last minute.

Makes approximately 20 puffs.

Crabmeat Delight.....

This is a delicious cold dip, but it is equally good piled high on toast rounds and heated in a hot oven (450°).

1 cup crabmeat
1/4 cup lime juice
3 oz. cream cheese
1/4 cup heavy cream
2 tbsps. mayonnaise
pinch salt

1 tbsp. minced onion
1 clove garlic, minced
1 tsp. finely chopped chives
2 dashes Tabasco
1 tsp. Worcestershire sauce

Marinate crabmeat in the lime juice for at least 1 hour. Whip the cream cheese and cream with electric mixer until mixture is smooth. Add mayonnaise and blend well. Add onion, chives, and garlic. Fold crabmeat into the cream. Add Tabasco and Worcestershire sauce.

Makes about 2 cups.

CRABMEAT *and* GRUYÈRE TREATS

*We urge you to try these.
They are simple to make
and sure to make a hit.*

*1 cup crabmeat
1/4 cup Gruyère cheese, grated
1 tbsp. Chablis (or any dry white wine)
1/2 tsp. salt
1 tbsp. mayonnaise*

Mix all ingredients together. Pile high on rounds of white bread which have been toasted on one side. Bake in 450° oven until hot.

These may be frozen and heated when needed.

Makes about 50 treats.

Grapefruit dip

Don't be fooled by the title. This is not for afternoon tea.

6 oz. cream cheese
8 drops Tabasco
1/2 tsp. Worcestershire sauce
1 1/2 tsps. lemon juice
1/2 grapefruit

Mix cream cheese, Tabasco, Worcestershire sauce, and lemon juice together until well blended and fluffy. Remove sections from grapefruit, cut them into small pieces and add to cheese mixture. Spoon mixture into grapefruit shell. Garnish with paprika and parsley. Place shell in dish and arrange cold, raw vegetables around shell. Cauliflower, celery strips, carrots, and cold cooked shrimp are good accompaniments to this dip.

The dip will keep for several days in refrigerator.

Makes about 3/4 cup.

Hawaiian TERIYAKI

*This is similar to Japanese Teriyaki,
but it is made with beef rather than
fish. A man's dish.*

*1 lb. beef steak, preferably
sirloin*
1/4 cup soy sauce (see p. 54)
1 tbsp. sugar

1 clove garlic, minced
*1 tbsp. minced fresh ginger
(or 1/8 tsp. powdered ginger)*

Cut steak into 1-inch cubes. Combine remaining ingredients. Marinate steak in sauce for at least 1 hour. Place 1 or 2 cubes on bamboo skewers and broil about 5 minutes on each side. If you can broil over charcoal, so much the better.

Makes approximately 40 cubes.

UNITED STATES 93

ice box
CHEESE WAFERS

Convenient to have for unexpected guests. Reminds us of cheese bits we ate when we were children.

> *1/2 lb. cheddar cheese, grated*
> *1/4 lb. butter*
> *1 1/2 cups sifted flour*
> *1/2 tsp. salt*
> *heavy pinch of cayenne pepper*

Combine cheese, butter, salt, and pepper. Cream well. Add flour. Form mixture into roll about 1 inch in diameter and wrap in waxed paper. Chill for about 2 hours. Slice roll into thin wafers and bake them in moderate oven (350°) for about 10 minutes, or until lightly browned. These wafers may be served hot or cold.

They may be kept in the refrigerator for about one week to be baked when needed, or they may be kept in the freezer, baked or unbaked.

Makes approximately 8 dozen wafers.

MAYONNAISE PUFFS

*The success of these puffs depends
upon the flavor of the onion.*

1 cup mayonnaise
2 egg whites, stiffly beaten
1/8 tsp. salt
1/4 tsp. Worcestershire sauce
2 medium onions, sliced
rounds of bread, toasted

Beat egg whites with salt until stiff. Fold in mayonnaise and Worcestershire sauce. Place thin slice of onion on each round of bread. Top each with a generous layer of mayonnaise mixture. Place under moderate flame for about 1 minute, or until mixture puffs and turns golden.

These may be reheated, but they are better served immediately. They may be prepared in advance, about 1 hour ahead of time, and put in the broiler when needed.

Makes about 36 puffs.

meat rolls in Blankets

Very popular. Filling may also be used with Liver Strudel dough (see page 21).

PASTRY:

1 cup sifted flour
1/2 tsp. salt

1/3 cup shortening
2–3 tbsps. cold water

Sift flour and salt together. Add shortening. Cut shortening until it is the size of small peas. Add the cold water and mix lightly with a fork until dough forms a ball. Do not handle too much. Chill.

FILLING:

1 cup cooked chicken
1/3 cup liverwurst
1 tbsp. butter
1 tbsp. catsup
1 egg yolk, beaten

1 egg white
1/2 tsp. salt
1/8 tsp. pepper
dash of cayenne
1 tbsp. Worcestershire sauce

Put chicken through finest blade of meat chopper twice. Add liverwurst and grind once more. Add remaining ingredients (except for egg yolk and white) and blend well.

Roll pie dough very thin. Cut into 2-inch squares. Make a roll of the filling about the size of your little finger and place it on one end of pastry square. Roll up until meat is completely enclosed. Seal roll with ▶

Olive CHEESE NUGGETS

Your guests will be surprised every time they bite into one of these tidbits. It's the olive that makes the difference.

1/4 lb. cheddar cheese, grated
1/4 cup butter
3/4 cup sifted flour
1/8 tsp. salt
1/2 tsp. paprika
36–40 medium stuffed olives

Blend butter and cheese. Add flour, salt, and paprika. Blend and mix well to form dough. Using about 1 teaspoonful of dough, flatten dough out in palm of your hand and wrap it around an olive. Place on ungreased baking sheet and bake in 400° oven 12 to 15 minutes, until light golden brown. Nuggets may be served hot or cold.

These may be made in advance and refrigerated before baking, or frozen baked or unbaked.

Makes about 36–40 nuggets.

✦ ✦ ✦

white of egg. Place rolls on cookie sheet, brush with beaten egg yolk, and bake in hot oven (450°) until brown, about 15 minutes.

The rolls can be prepared for baking the day before and kept in the refrigerator and baked when needed.

Makes approximately 36 rolls.

*These delightful roll-ups will please
any mushroom lover.*

1/2 cup sweet milk	*few grains black pepper*
1/2 cup chicken stock	*1 cup fresh mushrooms, sliced*
2 tbsps. butter	*1 tsp. lemon juice*
3 tbsps. flour	*10 thin slices fresh bread*
1/4 tsp. salt	*1/4 cup creamed butter*

Melt 2 tablespoons of butter in saucepan. Add flour and salt and stir until blended. Gradually add milk and chicken stock, stirring until thick. Clean mushrooms and sprinkle with salt, pepper, and lemon juice. Sauté in butter until tender. Add these to white sauce. Allow mixture to cool until ready to spread. Spread very thinly sliced bread (the fresher the bread the easier to roll) with mixture and roll up like a jelly roll. Secure each roll with a toothpick or string. Chill.

When ready to serve, spread each roll with the creamed butter, cut the roll into thirds, and bake in 350° oven until slightly brown. Garnish with a sprig of parsley.

These may be prepared in advance and refrigerated or frozen. Reheat before serving.

Makes about 30 sandwiches.

PEANUT BUTTER SURPRISE

A pleasant hors d'oeuvre made with ingredients you are likely to have on the pantry shelf.

1 can shrimp (approximately 36 small cooked shrimp)
1/4 cup peanut butter
3/4 cup mayonnaise
36 Ritz crackers

Soak shrimp in ice water for about 1 hour, if you use canned shrimp. Drain. Sprinkle with salt. Spread a thin layer of peanut butter on crackers. Spread a heavy layer (about 1 teaspoonful) of mayonnaise on top of peanut butter, making sure edges are covered. Place a small cooked shrimp in the middle. Broil under a moderate flame until mayonnaise begins to puff and is slightly golden.

These may be prepared in advance, refrigerated, and put under the broiler when needed.

Makes about 36 hors d'oeuvres.

Pseudo soufflés

This is an inexpensive hors d'oeuvre with a piquant flavor.

6 oz. cream cheese
2 tbsps. grated onion
2 tbsps. Worcestershire sauce
1/4 tsp. salt
1/8 tsp. pepper

1–2 tbsps. cream
12 slices bacon, partially cooked
12 very thin slices fresh bread

Mix cream cheese, onion, Worcestershire sauce, salt, and pepper together. Add enough cream to make mix spreadable. If regular sliced bread is used, slice it again. Bread should be very fresh and quite thinly sliced. Remove crusts. Spread cream cheese mixture on bread, roll tightly like a jelly roll. Wrap each roll in a piece of partially cooked bacon and secure with a toothpick. Chill. Remove from refrigerator, slice into 1-inch lengths, and bake in moderate oven (350°) until the bacon crisps. Serve warm.

These may be prepared in advance and frozen or refrigerated until ready to bake and serve.

Makes about 36 soufflés.

These are similar to fritters, but much better.

1 can tuna fish, drained and
    finely chopped
1 medium onion, finely chop-
    ped
4 tbsps. butter
3 tbsps. flour
1 cup milk

1/4 tsp. salt
1/8 tsp. pepper
1/2 cup flour
1/3 cup water
dash salt
2 egg whites, stiffly beaten

Sauté onion in 1 tablespoon of butter. Make a thick cream sauce with 3 tablespoons of butter, 3 tablespoons of flour, and the milk. Add tuna fish, onion, salt, and pepper. Chill for several hours.

Make a batter with 1/2 cup of flour and about 1/3 cup of water. The consistency should be like thin pancake batter. Add salt and fold in 2 beaten egg whites. Form balls about the size of large marbles out of the tuna mixture and roll balls in batter. Fry for a few seconds in very hot fat. Drain.

If you do not fry these too long, they may be made several hours in advance and reheated in a 400° oven for about 10 minutes when ready to serve. They must be served hot.

Makes approximately 48 puffs.

ACKNOWLEDGMENTS

A constant problem of the Women's Club of the United States Embassy, Tokyo, as with most private charitable organizations, has been the raising of funds for its philanthropic activities. It was believed that the sale of an hors d'oeuvres cookbook, in addition to raising funds, would serve to fill a real need, since finding new and different ideas for serving tempting snacks at cocktail parties appears to be a widespread problem for hostesses. It was therefore decided to collect the favorite hors d'oeuvres recipes from the many people at the Embassy, who had traveled and lived in the four corners of the globe.

Over a period of many months all the women connected with the U.S. Embassy in Tokyo were urged to submit their favorite hors d'oeuvres recipes to a special committee. The committee members tested each recipe submitted for flavor (our decisions were entirely subjective), for accurate measurements (a bit of this and a bit of that had to be translated into more standardized units of measure), for quantity (would it serve five or fifty), and for ease of preparation. In several instances more than one version of the same recipe was submitted. In such cases the committee took the liberty of either choosing the version it preferred or of combining the best features of the various submissions. The recipes were then written up to make·them consistent in form and style.

We wish to thank the following people for submitting their favorite recipes (which in some cases up to now have been closely guarded secrets) for publication in this book.

Mrs. Andrew Andranovich
Mrs. Conrad W. Anner
Mrs. La Verne Baldwin
Mrs. John Bernheim
Mrs. Arthur F. Blaser, Jr.
Mrs. Edward A. Bolster
Mrs. George V. Bowers
Mrs. Robert F. Brandt
Mrs. Harlan B. Clark
Miss Ellen J. Condas
Mrs. William F. DeMyer
Mrs. Richard A. Ericson, Jr.
Mrs. Joseph S. Evans, Jr.
Mrs. Philip F. Fendig
Mrs. Richard W. Finch
Mrs. Arnold Fraleigh
Mrs. Richard L. Goodrich
Mrs. James A. Griffin
Mrs. Martin F. Herz
Mrs. John M. Higgins
Mrs. John P. Horgan
Mrs. Outerbridge Horsey

Mrs. Leonard A. Humphreys
Mrs. Alfred Johnson
Mrs. Warren S. Lamour
Mrs. Christian H. Lunde-
gaard
Mrs. George A. Morgan
Mrs. Florence B. Nickerson
Mrs. Edwin T. Nishimura
Mrs. Sylvester I. Olson
Mrs. Gene W. Palmer
Mrs. Paul E. Pauly
Mrs. Paul J. Rappaport
Miss Stelia V. Ratto
Mrs. G. Edward Reynolds
Mrs. Paul A. Roessler
Mrs. William J. Schock
Mrs. Edward M. Skagen
Mrs. Richard L. Sneider
Mrs. Ben H. Thibodeaux
Mrs. Philip H. Trezise
Mrs. Ofelia S. Vargas

"BOOKS TO SPAN
THE EAST AND WEST"

RECIPES FROM THE EAST by Irma Walker Ross

MRS. MA'S CHINESE COOKBOOK by Nancy Chih Ma

CHINESE COOKING MADE EASY by Rosy Tseng

HAWAIIAN CUISINE: A Collection of Recipes from Members of the Hawaii State Society of Washington, D.C., featuring Hawaiian, Chinese, Japanese, Korean, Filipino, Portuguese, and cosmopolitan dishes.

CHOW: Secrets of Chinese Cooking by Dolly Chow

THE ART OF KOREAN COOKING by Harriett Morris

IN A PERSIAN KITCHEN: Favorite Recipes from the Near East by Maideh Mazda

JAPANESE FOOD AND COOKING by Stuart Griffin

RICE & SPICE: Rice Recipes from East to West by Phyllis Jervey

THE ART OF CHINESE COOKING by the Benedictine Sisters of Peking, founders of the famous Chinese cooking school in Tokyo.

A WORLD OF PARTIES: The Busy Germet's Guide to Exciting Entertaining by Phyllis Jervey

CHARLES E. TUTTLE COMPANY: PUBLISHERS
Rutland, Vermont & Tokyo, Japan